Churburg Castle

Dynastic residence and armoury

Helmut Stampfer
Translation: Joseph Swann

SCHNELL + STEINER

Foreword

The feudal period, when for generations a castle was the sole residence of a noble family, has faded into the past. Today castles, mansions and stately homes are, on the one hand, important historical and architectural sites for the country, state or region in which they are located; on the other they are at the focal point of increasing public interest in the conservation of the past and its artefacts. The personal and financial commitment of the owners of such landmarked buildings is more crucial than ever for the preservation of the ongoing family history and tradition to which they bear witness.

My own life, from childhood on, has been closely affected by the joys and responsibilities of castle dwellers. I grew up in the years following the Second World War surrounded by the romantic walls and spartan discomfort of Friedberg Castle in the Lower Inn Valley. As state conservation officer for the Tyrol, my father, Count Oswald Trapp, instilled in me an interest in castles, fortresses and ruins of all sorts, and in 1983, upon the death of my uncle Count Hans Trapp, I inherited Churburg Castle, rich in tradition, in the Upper Vinschgau (Venosta Valley). Thus I became responsible for one of the world's leading collections of medieval armour and weaponry, and for an extensive archive of the Tyrolian peerage reaching back to 1198. Ancient deeds and documents became a regular constituent of my annual stay within these walls.

We have been fortunate in gaining the services of our longstanding and esteemed state conservation officer, Dr. Helmut Stampfer, a recognized authority in these matters, as author of this guide, and it is to him that my warmest thanks are due. I must also thank the coordinators of this booklet, the South Tyrolean Castles Association, in the person of their president, Dr. Carl Philipp Baron von Hohenbühel. After publications on Taufers and Schenna castles, and on the Trostburg at Waidbruck (Ponte Gardena), it is now the turn of Churburg Castle, the Vinschgau's most significant secular monument, to appear in print. My thanks are likewise due to the publishers, Schnell & Steiner, who in the late 1950s first produced the short guide to Churburg Castle written by my father, Count Oswald Trapp.

I hope this new guidebook will give you, its readers, much pleasure as well as information, and I wish you a wealth of new impressions and knowledge in exploring its pages.

Count Johannes J. Trapp
Churburg, April 2015

History

The historian Franz Huter considered the Vinschgau (Venosta Valley), from the source of the River Etsch (Adige) to the glacial step at Töll above Merano, as the original core of the Tyrol. Here, in the Upper Vinschgau – the stretch between Reschen (Resia) and Schluderns (Sluderno) – the unique blend of natural and cultural landscape peculiar to this region attains its climax. To the north the lakes below the pass, and to the south the glacial Ortler range form the natural boundaries of the wide valley, whose geographical routes lead not only south-east along the course of the Etsch, but also south-west over the Umbrail Pass into Lombardy, and west across the Fuorn Pass into the Engadine. The area thus always offered excellent access and communications, and its settlement from the

View of Churburg Castle 1881

HISTORY

Bronze Age onwards has been documented by finds at the Tartscher Bichl, a glacially eroded rock formation between Mals and Schluderns, and especially on the Ganglegg Ridge north of Schluderns. That the valley was, even in pre-Roman times, part of a long-distance transportation artery has been confirmed by the recent discovery of a staging post south of the Haider See, which was active from the first century BC until the seventh century AD. The small Roman objects found there, as well as the fine mid-first-century AD Greek marble head of Venus discovered a few years ago at Mals, shed new light upon the importance of the Via Claudia Augusta, which connected Rome with the north via the Reschen Pass.

After the fall of the Roman Empire, the bishops of Chur, whose diocese took in much of the Vinschgau, assumed secular as well as spiritual authority over the region. The importance of the connection between the Franconian territories in the north and Lombardy in the south grew after Charlemagne's defeat of the Lombards in 774. It is no coincidence, therefore, that the churches in both Mals and Müstair rank artistically and architecturally among the most important of all Carolingian monuments. The ancient belief that Müstair was founded personally by Charlemagne has, in fact, gained credence from recent archaeological and dendrochronological (tree-dating) research in the church and abbey buildings. The Vinschgau was incorporated into the Holy Roman Empire, and the Carolingian system of counties already introduced, during Charlemagne's lifetime. Later, towards the end of the high Middle Ages, various noble families like the Matsch and the Counts of Tyrol successfully extended their power at the expense of the bishops of Chur and Trent.

The death of Emperor Frederick II in 1250 left a dangerous vacuum at the centre of power, with manifold local repercussions. Thus at the conclusion of a feud between the Bishop of Chur, Henry IV de Montfort, and the lords of Matsch and Wangen, the bishop was granted the right in 1253 to build a castle or fortress between Cleven and Latsch *at whatsoever place he desire*. Given the insecurity of the age, the bishop, whose base in the Upper Vinschgau had so far been at Müstair Abbey, took immediate advantage of this right and commissioned a new purpose-built stronghold. A deed issued by

pp. 4–5:
View from south-west: the medieval core of the castle, with great hall on the left and keep on the right, on the summit of the small hill, dates from the sixth decade of the 13th century; outbuildings, garden terraces to the south, and dove tower (bottom right) were added in the 16th century.

pp. 8–9:
View from north-west: (l. to r.) keep, north wing, great hall, front gate tower; (bottom right) Pfaffeneck Tower.

Churburg Castle from the north with the Ortler in the background

Bishop Henry IV at Churburg on February 21, 1259 – the first documentary mention of the castle – indicates that he had taken up residence by this date. The castle's position at the threshold of the Matsch (Mazia) Valley, where the Matsch family owned castles at Upper and Lower Matsch, constituted an unmistakable signal on the part of the bishop. The ambitious Matsch clan, which had not only acquired extensive estates north and south of the Alps but had also gained the reeveship (supervisory authority) over the Benedictine abbey of Marienberg, founded in 1146, was to be put firmly in its place. However, Henry's successors did not long benefit from his strategic ploy. Less than 40 years later, in 1297, Churburg Castle itself was in the hands of the Matsch family. In the course of the 14th century the various branches of that clan destroyed each other in bouts of violent feuding, and by 1348 the hitherto feudally liege-free

Matsch were obliged to accept the overlordship of the Bavarian ruler, Louis of Brandenburg, second husband of the Tyrolean heiress Margarethe Maultasch. They were, however, allowed to retain their lands in fief, and Ulrich IV von Matsch had by 1361 achieved the position of governor of the Etsch and the rank of burgrave of the Tyrol. In the following century the fortunes of the family revived, only to come to an abrupt end with Gaudenz, the last of the male line. This vivid personality was governor of the Etsch from 1478–1482 and major domo to the Tyrolean regent Archduke Sigmund the Rich in Coin. He fell into disfavour and suffered banishment for his unexpected retreat in the face of the Venetian forces at the Battle of Calliano (1487), but was later pardoned – though never again trusted – by Emperor Maximilian I. Gaudenz died in poverty at Churburg in 1504. His nephews Jakob V, Karl and Georg Trapp, sons of his sister Barbara, bore the cost of a funeral befitting their uncle's position, and the bishop of Chur thereupon made over half the castle to the brothers in fief.

Their father, Jakob IV, was the first of the Trapp family to move from Styria to the Tyrol, where he rose to high position in the service of Archduke Sigmund. In 1452 the Archduke sent him to Milan to observe the latest developments in the manufacture of armour, and in 1469 appointed him hereditary major domo. Jakob IV died in 1475; the parish church of Bozen (Bolzano) contains a gravestone bearing his arms.

After Gaudenz's death, his son-in-law, Erhard von Polheim, laid claim to the other half of Churburg Castle. This gave rise to lengthy disputes that were only resolved 33 years later in a settlement that established the Trapp brothers' right to the whole castle – a right ratified in the enfeoffment of the disputed half in 1541. Since then, this unique cultural monument has been in the unbroken possession of the Trapp family who continue to maintain it in exemplary fashion as their country seat in the Upper Vinschgau.

Situation and architectural history

A rare gem of the locality (Schluderns), and of the vale itself in all its length and breadth, is the fine chivalric castle of Churburg, whose clear elevations, set upon a modest hill, rise amid a garland of fruit trees above the south-eastern borders of the village.

Here is the summer residence of the owners, the family of the Counts of Trapp. The castle contains valuable archives, in which its own history and

Pathway up to front castle gate ▷
from the west

SITUATION AND ARCHITECTURAL HISTORY

that of the surrounding region is preserved, as well as an interesting collection of ancient armour and knightly weaponry.
Johann Jakob Staffler's florid description marks the entrance of Churburg into the annals of regional research. The reference to archives and armour, however, is as valid today as it was in 1841.
The castle stands in a naturally exposed position on a hill above Schluderns. The original buildings were laid down on an east-west axis, the south-eastern and south-western slopes only being incorporated later. Surrounded by a curtain wall, the original complex consisted of the great hall to the west, the keep to the east, and the old chapel to the south-east. No prehistoric or early remains have been discovered. The oldest drawing, dating from the early 16th century, shows the keep with its characteristically splayed crown – a defensive device, based probably on Italian models, unique in the Tyrol. The pyramidal roof to the keep was removed by Count Gotthard as a precaution against fire in 1892. Around 1500 the west façade of the great hall evidently still contained a row of Romanesque double-arched windows suggestive of a banqueting hall. A further original element of the ensemble is Pfaffeneck Tower, set below the castle at the approach from the village of Schluderns. Destroyed in the mid-14th century feuds between the various branches of the Bailiffs of Matsch, it was restored in 1537 and later used as a gunpowder store.
The only extant evidence of the buildings erected in the 14th to 15th centuries is a number of isolated architectural features. The following century, however, saw major changes, in the course of which the castle took on the basic appearance it still has today. The first building phase, from c. 1510–1544, comprised the refurbishment of the great hall, the building of a new north wing and a second new block to the east of the keep, the raising of the curtain wall, and the construction of a two-winged loggia. All of this work was in the late Gothic style of the reign of Emperor Maximilian I – indeed the Emperor himself visited Churburg in 1516 – whereas the present-day arcaded courtyard with its decorated vaulting embodies the new Mannerist ideas of the 1570–1580 decade, which are also evident in Jakob's Room from the same period. These changes transformed the medieval stronghold into a richly appointed Renaissance castle where defence and display went hand in hand. That the former was still relevant, however, is evident from Marx Sittich von Wolkenstein's description of Churburg around 1600 as a frontier post against the *Engadeiner* and *Graubindner* from across the Swiss border.

Outer courtyard ▷
with the Tree Room

Guide to the Castle

A broad flight of steps leads up from the car park to what is today the **main castle gate** at the south-west corner of the old complex. There was always an entrance here, but the present crenellated gate tower dates from the first half of the 16th century; the murals on its entrance and courtyard façades are from 1557. The old round-arched doorway and the window above it were originally framed with elaborately worked trompe l'oeil pilasters and beams in dark grey Renaissance style, but this decoration is so weathered that it is now hardly visible. On the architrave stand two figures bearing the arms of the lords of the castle. Clad in armour, they wear the typical skirt and plumed helm of the mid-16th century and hold a tilting lance or small standard in their free hand. As well as the Trapp quarterings, the arms show in the inescutcheon the three wings of the Matsch, an augmentation granted in 1555 by King Ferdinand I.

Passing through the castle gate, one sees on the right the **summer house**, which looks onto the **terraced gardens**. Laid out in the mid-16th century, these extend to the more recent lower encircling wall, which ends in a small **tower**, whose architectural purpose is manifestly

Outer courtyard looking east with bell tower on right

Painting commemorating the first ascent of the Ortler by Josef Pichler, the Churburg gamekeeper, in 1804

The painting on the ground floor of the inner courtyard shows Churburg Castle set in majestic mountain scenery culminating in the Ortler, at 3905 m the highest peak of the Tyrol, with a group of three men – one of whom demonstratively points the way forward – in the foreground. An inscription relates that on September 27, 1804 Josef Pichler, the Churburg gamekeeper, completed the first ascent of the Ortler. Pichler hailed from St. Leonhard in Passeier, and was for that reason known as "Pseirer Josele". For many years he occupied the panelled room at the east of the courtyard, which is still called the Jägerstüberl (Hunters' Room). After the conquest of the Grossglockner in 1800, Archduke Johann had entrusted J. Gebhard, an officer, with finding a way up the Ortler. After several attempts, Pseirer Josele and his two companions from the Zillertal succeeded in their climb – illness having confined Gebhard to the valley. Setting out from Trafoi shortly after midnight, they reached the peak in the course of the morning, and by eight o'clock in the evening had returned to their starting point in the best of spirits. The route they chose, via the so-called Hintere Wandlen to the Oberer Ortlerferner, is still today considered one of the more difficult and dangerous approaches.

Arcaded Renaissance quadrangle (c. 1570)

decorative rather than defensive. Like the tower at Goldrain Castle near Latsch in the Vinschgau, it actually contains dovecotes in its upper storey. Its façade decoration of trompe l'oeil architectural motifs and divisions, with the arms of the Trapp and related families, and a Jerusalem Cross referring to the pilgrimage undertaken by Jakob VII, was accomplished in 1562–63. The bottom terrace now also contains the **Amor fountain**, placed there some decades ago, as its original location – perhaps the arcaded courtyard – could no longer be determined. Familiar from classical mythology, the young god of love with his drawn bow was most likely made from a cast by Gilg Sesselschreiber, who had worked on the Emperor Maximilian's tomb in Innsbruck. The small bronze statue – the original of which is now kept in a showcase in Matsch Hall – is a fine example of early Renaissance sculpture. The statue now on the fountain is a copy by the Vinschgau artist Karl Grasser.

The cobbled **outer courtyard** rises past the end of the former **great hall**, to which a large rectangular bay bearing a coat of arms was added in 1518, through the **rounded arch** beneath the so-called Tree Room – a more recent addition bridging the courtyard – into the **arcaded courtyard**. Directly opposite the entrance hangs a carved and

Western arcade of the loggia ▷

GUIDE TO THE CASTLE

North-west corner pillar (herm) of loggia

coloured wooden roundel displaying the full Trapp **coat of arms** framed in a laurel wreath. What is only faintly discernible on the gate tower façade can now be clearly seen for the first time: the original Trapp arms in the form of a double broken red bar, with the later addition of a bustard (Ger. *Trappe*) as a heraldic motif expressive of the family name, and finally the inescutcheon of the extinct Matsch line, three blue wings in silver, added in 1555.

Arcaded courtyard

Crossing the threshold into the arcaded courtyard, one is immediately captivated by its atmosphere. This is no longer merely painted architecture, as at the gate tower: it is the real thing – Renaissance architecture set in a medieval castle. Above a series of wide, but unevenly arched openings at courtyard level extends an Italianate loggia with an arcade of five round arches looking onto the courtyard on each long, and three on each short side. The loggia was built in two stages. According to a report of 1537 a *fine gallant vaulted passage* was already added to the new north wing and part of the great hall during the lifetime of Jakob V (†1533). This early loggia, with its two unevenly long sides, is comparable with the arcade built in 1517 in the courtyard of Prösels Castle, though this has pointed arches set on elegant octagonal sandstone pillars, whereas Churburg, in accordance with Vinschgau tradition, has short **marble pillars** delicately worked in the late (and by then declining) Gothic style. Examples of this early work are the fourth pillar (with the Wolkenstein arms) in the east arcade, the second (with the Trapp arms) in the north, and the fifth (also with the Trapp arms) in the west arcade. The stonemason's mark on these carvings – repeated on the coat of arms of 1518 and on a window in the north wing of the castle – indicates that they are the work of Oswald Furter from Latsch, active at Churburg from 1518. A second mason from Latsch, Kaspar Reuter, whose mark can be seen on the third pillar (with the Matsch arms) of the north and the fourth (with the Tannberg arms) of the west arcade worked with him. These five pillars are typically late

Late Gothic arcade pillar

North-east corner pillar (herm) of loggia

Gothic, even if dolphins – a Renaissance innovation – make a solitary appearance.
The present loggia, with its **four arcades** surrounding a central courtyard, was not built until the 1570s. Accordingly, the **remaining pillars**, and above all those at the **corners** – so-called **herms** in the form of (or with the heads of) gods or other figures – have broken with the late Gothic tradition and breathe the quite different spirit of Mannerism. Extant documents attribute these works to the master sculptor-stonemasons Valthin and Wolf Kolb. As the older pillars are not all in the same row but interspersed with the new, it is clear that the original loggia was not extended in the second building phase, but demolished and completely rebuilt. Starting at the north-west corner, each pillar bears a **coat of arms** which, together with its neighbour in clockwise order, signifies a Trapp marriage. The oldest of these pairings refers to the marriage of Jakob IV with Barbara von Matsch in 1462, which established the rights of the Trapp line to the castle. The latest pairing, commemorating the mar-

GUIDE TO THE CASTLE

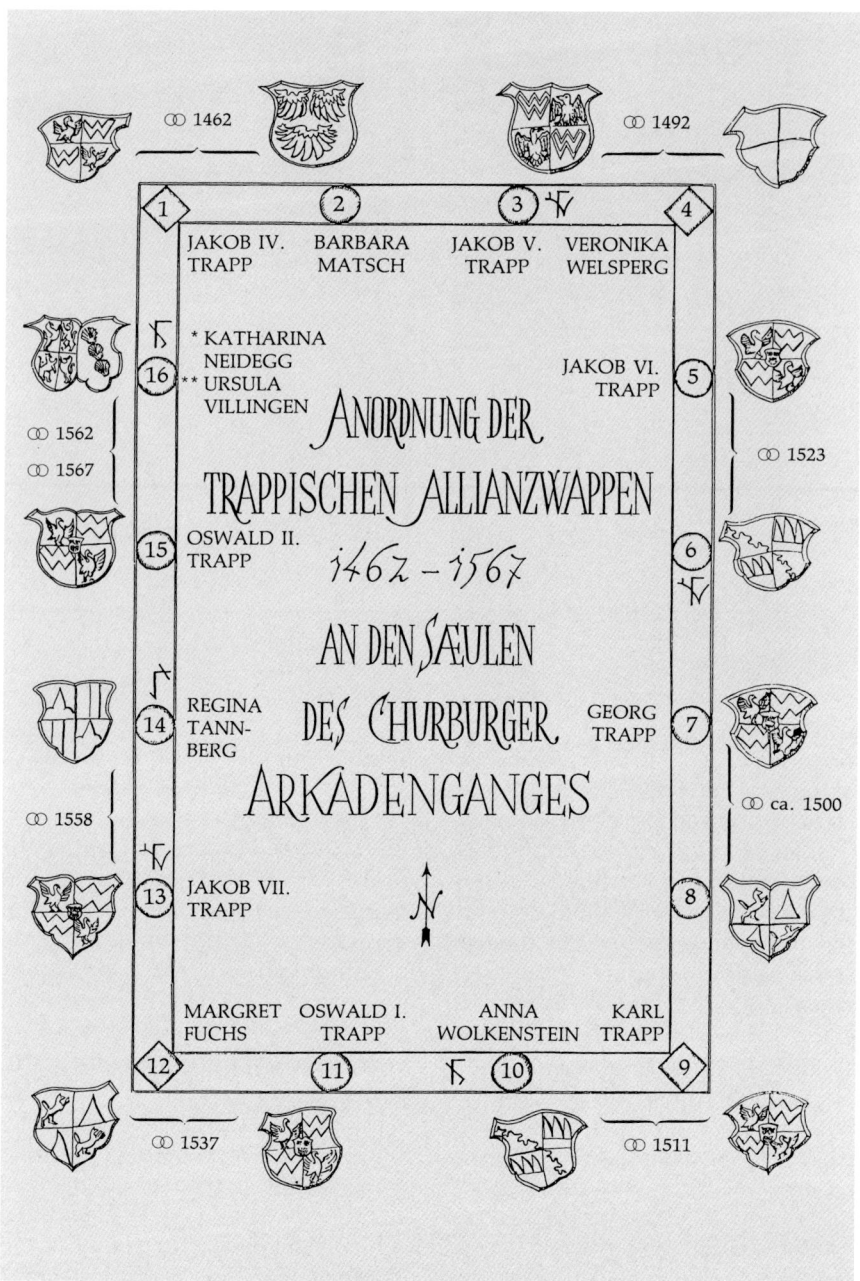

Order of pillars and coats of arms in the loggia

Mythical progenitor of the Lords of Matsch (1171)

riage of Oswald II and Ursula von Villingen in 1567, can serve as a basis for dating the present loggia. The striking variety of these pillars – whether from the third or eighth decade of the 16th century – lends the arcaded courtyard a special flair, setting it apart from other Renaissance loggias of the Tyrol. The arcades of Ehrenburg in the Pustertal (c. 1522) and Dornsberg in the Vinschgau (1535–1540), for example, though somewhat earlier, are more consistently of the Renaissance. Churburg is unique in its juxtaposition, under its round arches, of late Gothic and Mannerist forms. Imported from gentler regions, the loggia architecture might well be thought inappropriate to the climate of the Upper Vinschgau, but Churburg's arcades have nevertheless been spared the addition of modern glazing imposed elsewhere on functional grounds.

The catalogue of dynastic unions cut in the marble of the arcade pillars continues in the medium of paint on the loggia vault and walls. The entire ceiling is decorated with the fruits, leaves and branches of a single tree, not merely as a topical motif – the roof of foliage, beloved of the Renaissance, uniting the human dwelling with the universe – but as the symbolic genealogical tree of the Trapp family and their

Loggia: cock and wolf

forefathers, the Lords of Matsch. The roots of this tree can be traced back to the south wall where, next to a deep-set window niche whose surround bears the arms of the Tyrolean regent Archduke Ferdinand II, the mythical patriarch of the clan, **Laurentius von Matsch** (1171) reclines, clad in the armour of the Renaissance, his helm with

Loggia: horse and lion

its panache of feathers next to him, his sword and the arms of the Matsch-Colonna families hanging from the tree-trunk above. From his breast – reminiscent of the Christian iconography of the root of Jesse – the tree spreads its arms up and out into the loggia vault. Scattered between the leaves and fruits of the many branches are coats of arms and inscriptions relating the succession of main and subordinate family lines. The coloured ribs of the vault interrupt the continuity of the depiction, but at the same time emphasize the Gothic elements of the architecture. A series of famous Roman heads on the **vault brackets** leads the eye to the **wall paintings**, which in turn reveal a programmatic enthusiasm for antiquity.

Above the red and white patterned dado, with its allusion to the Trapp

Loggia: a big fool hatches little fools

colours, various **animals** from Aesop's fables – fox and crow, wolf and crane, monkey and peacock, horse and lion – as well as other **fabulous creatures** strut and pose

Loggia: little fools are stuffed into sacks

on a trompe l'oeil ledge. The idea may have come from the slightly older (c. 1565) depiction of animals and grotesque creatures in the north wing of Ambras Castle, near Innsbruck. Transformed by the Tyrolean regent Ferdinand II into the most important late Renaissance edifice of the Tyrol, the castle served as a model for many members of the regional nobility. The Churburg murals are also, however, related to the episcopal Castel del Buonconsiglio in Trent, where the artist Dosso Dossi decorated the dining hall – known as the *Stua de la famea* – of Cardinal Bernhard von Cles with ten of Aesop's fables set in wide landscapes. A series of images on the **south wall** of the loggia devoted to **fools and folly** interrupts the classical tone. Possibly connected with Thomas Murner's critique of Luther (1522), they nevertheless continue the didactic thrust of the fables. The humanistic educational ideal reaches its climax in the sequence of **24 Latin mottos** inscribed on ornately framed tablets. Alongside the texts of famous classical philosophers (Aristotle, Heraclitus, Thales) are others from the Church fathers (Basil, Evagrius), and even biblical passages from the Book of Sirach (Ecclesiasticus). This is also the source of the motto to the right above the entrance to Jakob's Room *Laudemus viros gloriosos et parentes nostros in generatione sua* (*Let us praise the men of glory, our fathers in their generation*) – a most suitable text for the starting point of a genealogical tree. The didactic intention of the loggia's pictorial programme, with its consistent emphasis on the values of family, moderation and wisdom, was not uncommon at the time. Similar mottos from the same period can be found in the "philosophers' passage" at Maretsch Castle in Bozen, or in Jöchelsthurn, a stately home at Sterzing (Vipiteno), as well as in the "Antiquarium" of Munich's Residenz palace.

The reveals (side-faces) of a wide wall niche at the southern end of the west arcade provide a hint as to the maker of these murals. Two symmetrical putti hold the shield of the artists' guild on the left hand side and a crowned helm with a crest in the form of a bust and antlers on the right. Between them is a basket of fruit, together with a compass, two palettes, a ruler and mahlstick, and in the peak of the arch a bag of tracing charcoal – the various tools of the artist's trade. The pre-1581 work on the loggia has traditionally been credited to a certain Paul, who was paid for completing various paintings at the castle – unfortunately not described in any detail – between 1576 and 1581. He is probably identical with Paul Morizius, described in 1582 as *maller auf Curburg* (*painter at Churburg*), who has recently been linked by Leo Andergassen to Paolo Naurizio, an artist active from 1583–1597 in the Trentino region, whose father had come from Nuremberg to Trent – hence the surname Nauritius (the

West arcade:

15. ABSVRDVM EST SEQVENTEM HONORES / FVGERE LABORES. EX QVIBUS NASCVNTVR / HONORES. EVAGRIVS.
    (It is absurd for one who seeks honours to flee the work that leads to them. Evagrius)

16. MAXIMA EST DIGNITAS NON QVIDEM / VTI HONORIBVS. SED EFFICERE VT DIGNVS ILLIS EXISTIMERE / ARISTOTELES.
    (The greatest value is not to possess honours but to ensure that you are held worthy of them. Aristotle)

17. NVLLVS LAVDEM VO[LVPTATE] COMPARAVIT / SED LABORES PARIVN[T NOBILEM] FORTITV/DINEM ISOCRATES.
    (None has ever compared praise with pleasure, but labour bears fruit in noble constancy. Isocrates)

18. BEATVS CVIVS VITA EXCELSA EST, ET SPIRITVS HVMILIS. NILVS.
    (Blessed the man of eminent life who remains humble of heart. Nilus)

19. NOBILES ET PVLCHROS MAXIME DECET IN ASPEC/TV PVLCHRITVDO, IN ANIMO AVTEM TEMPERANTIA, / ET IN HORVM VTROQ(VE) FORTITVDO ET VIRILITAS. / DEMOSTHENES.
    (Beauty of aspect well befits the noble and the refined, so long as they possess modesty of heart, together with constancy and manliness. Demosthenes)

20. ANIMI LAVDEM IACTATO, NON MAIORVM EMOR/TVAM GLORIAM. P. PIALARIDES.
    (Praise the spirit of your forefathers, not their bygone glory. P. Phalarides)

21. GENEROSOS ESSE PVTATO NON QVI A BONIS / ET PROBIS P(RO)CREATI SVNT, SED QVI BONI/TATEM ET PROBITATEM P(RO)FITENTVR. THEOPOMPVS.
    (Think not those noble who are born of good and upright family, but who profess goodness and uprightness. Theopompus)

7. QVALEM PARENTIBVS RETVLERIS / GRATIAM, TALEM A LIBERIS EXPECTATO. MILESIVS PHILOSOPHVS.
   (The love you give your parents you can expect from your children. Milesius)

8. QVORVM LAVDES MAGNI AESTIMAS, ILLORVM ETIAM VIRTVTES AEMVLERIS. ISOCRATES PHILOSSOPHVS.
   (Emulate the virtue of those whose merits you esteem. Isocrates)

9. On the stairway to Matsch Hall:
   VIAM ET GLORIAM MAXIME COM/PENDIARIAM, SI QVIS BONVS ESSE / STVDERET, DICEBAT HERACLITVS PHILOSSOPHVS.
   (The way and the glory are nearest when one strives for goodness, said the philosopher Heraclitus)

10. DIFFICILE EST FATEOR. SED TEN/DIT AD ERDVA VIRTVS. / ET TALIS MERITI GRATIA MAIOR ERIT. OVIDIVS.
    (That it is difficult I admit, but virtue strives for higher things, and so much the greater will be the reward for that merit. Ovid)

11. VIRTVTIS MAGIS QVAM CORPORIS / IMMAGINES AC MONVMENTA RELIN/QVENDA QVTATO / ISOCRATES PELVS.
    (Esteem virtue more highly than appearances and monuments. Isocrates)

12. TVRPE EST [IN ALIIS VIR]TVTES APPROBARE [ET IN]SEIPSIS VITIA / HABERE / NACTES PH[ILOSOPH]VS.
    (It is base to praise the virtue of others and cultivate vice in oneself. Nactes / Hipponax)

13. BONORVM VIRORVM RELIQVIAS / TEMPVS NON ABOLET SED ETIAM / DEFVNCTIS EIS VIRTVS RELVCET / EVRIPIDES.
    (Time does not pale the memory of the pure. Even when they are dead their virtue shines on. Euripides)

14. [LIBEROS] DOCTIORES QVAM / [DITIORES] RELINQVERE STVDETO / [EPIC]TETVS.
    (Strive to leave wise rather than rich children. Epictetus)

Latin mottos in the loggia arcades

1. Above the entrance to Jakob's Room:
   LAVDEMVS VIROS GLORIOSOS ET PA/RENTES NOSTROS IN GENERATIONE SVA. / ECCTI XXXXIIII.
   (Let us now praise famous men, and our fathers in their generations. Sirach 44.1)

2. MORTVVS EST PATER EIVS ET QVASI NO(N) / EST MORTVVS. RELIQVIT ENIM DEFENSOREM / DOMVS CONTRA INIMICOS ET AMICIS / REDDENTEM GRATIAM. ECCLESIASTICI XXX.
   (The father may die, and yet he is not dead, for he has left behind him an avenger against his enemies, and one to repay the kindness of his friends. Sirach 30.4,6)

3. Above the window in Jakob's Room:
   LIBERI [GRATI] MAGNAS EFFIC[IV]NT PARENTVM LAVDATIONES / LIBERI INSIPIENTIA ET INPERITIA EXVLTANTES COGNATIONIS / SVAE GENEROSITATEM CONTAMINANT. BASILIVS.
   (Grateful children bring honour upon their parents; children that exult in shallowness and folly bring their noble family into disrepute. Basil)

4. LAVDABILIS PIETAS EST. VT EOS QVI NOS / PROCREARVNT HONORE IFFICTIMVS, ET LABORES / EORVM REMVNEREMVS CYRILLVS.
   (Respect is praiseworthy – that we should honour our parents and repay their labours. Cyril)

5. NON IDCIRCO EQVVS EST CELER, SI. EX / CELERRIMIS NATVS SIT. SIC VIRI LAVDES / TESTATE SVNT EX SVIS CVIVSQ(VE) PRAECLA/RIS FACTIS. S. BASILIVS.
   (A horse is not fast because its parents were fast. A man's praise rests on his own noble deeds. Basil)

6. TALEM TE PRAESTA PARENTIBVS / QVALES ERGA TE CVPIS ESSE TVOS / LIBEROS. ISOCRATES PHILOSSOPHVS.
   (Serve your parents as you would wish your own children to serve you. Isocrates)

Loggia: peacock with inscription

Nuremberger). Among other works of his is an altarpiece for Trent cathedral (now in the diocesan museum) commissioned by Oswald Trapp II. That he is explicitly mentioned in the records (where the M instead of an N is probably a scribal error), and that he is known to have worked for the Trapp family strongly suggests that the Churburg murals are also his work, even if their obliteration with limewash in the 18th century and restoration in 1907–1908 make direct stylistic comparison with Nauritius' other work impossible. Most of his work in the Trentino is in any case religious; however, he (or his school) has recently been held responsible for the allegories of time and the seasons, with the four divisions of the earth, the winds, and two virtues that adorn the great hall of the Palazzo Lodron in Trent – a sequence dated 1583. The most recent phase of renovation of the Churburg loggia has revealed further aspects of the murals, and in general restored and secured them for future generations.

Turkey with woman's head

pp. 32–33: General view of Jakob's Room

22. … RVM NOBILITATEM N … / LVTVM ENIM OMNES … LNER … /
ET QVI IN PVRPVRA ET BYSSO SVNT EDVCATI, ET QVI / IN PAVPERTATIS
ABYSSO QSVMPTI THESPIS.
(… not only those brought up in purple and fine linen, but also those caught in the depths of poverty. Thespis)

23. APELLES PICTOR INTERROGATVS CVR / SEDENTEM PINXISSET
FORTVNAM QVIA / INQVIT, NON STAT.
(Asked why he painted the goddess Fortuna seated, the artist Apelles replied 'Because she never stands still'.)

24. Doorway to the Tree Room:
DIFFICILE EST SE NOSSE, SED BEATVM. / THALES.
(To know yourself is difficult, but blessed. Thales)

Taken from: Leo Andergassen, *Churburg – Geschichte, Gestalt und Kunst*, Verlag Schnell & Steiner GmbH, Munich/Zurich 1991, 35–38.

Motto from Demosthenes (19): Wolf and crane, fox and crow

Motto from Phalarides (20): Fool with bagpipes and wine glass

Motto from Heraclitus (9): Monkey with mirror, cat with candlestick

Motto from Hipponax (12): Ram and ewe, clad and decorated with feathers

Doorway from Jakob's Room to loggia

Jakob's Room

From the loggia a **door** with two inlaid panels showing landscapes adorned with ruins (the upper panel is dated 1572) opens into Jakob's Room, so called in honour of Jakob VII. Its former use as a dining room can be surmised from the busily cooking putti on the right reveal of the corridor window and the cupbearer and waiter on the wide doorway reveal. The lower part of this reveal shows an angel hovering

GUIDE TO THE CASTLE

Doorway from Jakob's Room to library

Jakob Trapp VII died at the youthful age of 34, but his life illustrates the characteristic stages in the biography of a nobleman of that period. Born in 1529 as the son of Jakob VI and Katharina Baroness Wolkenstein, he spent his childhood at Churburg. Later we encounter him as a student in Padua. At the age of 24 he received his first suit of armour, preserved in the Churburg armoury, which he wears in the portrait of 1555. In 1558 – the year of his father's death – he married Anna Regina von Tannberg from Upper Austria (at the time a province of Bavaria).

In 1559, the year in which his son Jakob VIII was born, Jakob VII commissioned a portable organ from Michael Strobel, a craftsman from Amberg, near Braunau on the Inn. A Latin inscription on the magnificent organ case celebrates his patronage. His love of music is also attested in three songbooks (Nuremberg 1538), which he annotated in Latin in 1544 and 1559. The portrait statue in wood dates from the same period. The pose and clothing show that this extremely rare work was made neither as an official memorial nor for representational purposes but purely as a private memento. Beseno Castle has a similarly full-scale figure of Oswald Trapp, dated 1569 – perhaps an indication of a family tradition in this matter. The story has it that the statue was carved by Jakob VII himself, but that is highly unlikely: the high quality of workmanship suggests the sculptor Wolf Verdross as its author. The life-size work may have been executed for the family in connection with Jakob's pilgrimage to the Holy Land in 1560. He left Beseno Castle on June 5 of that year and returned safe and sound on November 20, reaching the family home at Churburg four days later. Unfortunately, there is no written memoir of the more than six-month voyage, but Jakob's grey loden cape with the Jerusalem Cross stitched onto it can still be seen in the room named after him, along with the standing wooden statue and table organ – all of them invaluable treasures. One year after his return Jakob had the new chapel built at Churburg, and at the same time commissioned a family history, the *Historia und Annalpuech der Trappen* (*History and Annals of the Trapp Family*). In 1562 Wolf Verdross created a portrait medal of his patron, and about the same time Jakob had the dove tower built and decorated with heraldic and architectural motifs. In mid-June 1563 he set out for Innsbruck, where he died suddenly of spotted fever on July 5. Ten years later a magnificent monument in white marble, again by Wolf Verdross, depicting Jakob in full armour kneeling before the Cross, was erected over his grave in Schluderns parish church.

Dove tower (1562) ▷

Jupiter ceiling medallion in Jakob's Room

with a laurel wreath above the marital arms of the Matsch-Trapp, proclaiming the motto *Die Tugent liebn khrön ich hiemit / Diß ort den andern zimmet nit / Anno domini 1580* (*Love of virtue is my crown / All others here I do disown / AD 1580*). On the inside of the room the richly carved door frame may well have originally been coloured, but the colours were reduced during the Baroque period to white and gold. The frame is surmounted by an elaborate ornamental relief showing Jupiter, the father of the gods, seated on an eagle with outspread wings, while two female genies hold a laurel wreath over his head. With their free hand they touch the helmets of the Matsch arms, which are displayed on a shield held by two griffons at the base of the group. This outstanding example of the wood-carver's skill continues on the **door frame** itself, which is richly worked with Mannerist ornamentation and trophies, and finds its complement in the **door frame to the library**, above which is inscribed the motto *Recte faciendo neminem time* (*Do right and fear none*). Regrettably, the figure of Juno in the ornamental panel above the doorway must, to early 18th century tastes, have appeared rather too free with her charms; she was at all events replaced around that time with a decorative grille, while her attributes and the Trapp arms were left intact. Jupiter and Juno – as the two coats of arms clearly show – honour the bond of marriage between the Matsch and Trapp families. On the other hand Jupiter in particular – found in similar pose around 1550 in the murals at the Firmian Palace in Trent and in Valer Castle on the Nonsberg – also expresses the humanistic interest in mythology typical of the age. The same artist who worked on the door frames – in all probability Wolf Kolb – was responsible for the **ceiling brackets**, with their carved masks, and the **reliefs** on the deeply panelled ceiling itself. The three octagons on the central axis again show Jupiter between Sol and Luna, with around the edges the signs of the zodiac in demi-format, again finished in white and gold. Thus the annual cosmic cycle extended in a single continuum into the realms of astrology, anticipating the motif that Ferdinand II commissioned in 1586 in more elaborate form for the ceiling of the dining hall at Ambras Castle.

Triumph of Flora (May-June)

Superimposed on an older phase of painting (c. 1544), which is partly still preserved under the damask wall hangings of 1913, the room received its present aspect between 1576 and 1580. A **frieze** of six richly framed images depicts the seasons of the earth, two months at a time, each painting centred on an allegorical figure in a carriage or chariot, accompanied by an assembly of other personages bearing attributes and banners in triumphal procession. The January-February image shows Janus, the two-headed god of the year's beginning. Following him – and partly concealed behind the great tiled stove – is Plantator, the planter. May-June is dedicated to the triumph of flower-wreathed Flora, and the two summer months to the fertility goddess Ceres. September-October show Abundantia with her following, symbolizing

Triumph of Deus Venter (November-December), dated 1579

Figure of Jakob VII with pilgrim's cape (c. 1560)

Griffon's claw drinking vessel, buffalo horn (early 15th century)

the fullness of harvest-time. Finally Deus Venter, the personification of gluttony, makes his triumphant entry in November-December. Two further images are difficult to decipher, as they are partly obscured by the carved door-heads – one above the entrance to the library, where all that can clearly be seen is a ship, and the other above the entrance from the loggia, where only a lyre player is visible. The door frames must have been added after the

Table organ by Michael Strobel from Amberg near Braunau am Inn (1559)

painting was finished. The wall by the window shows a musician with a wind instrument, and the deep window reveal is decorated with three scenes from Ovid's *Metamorphoses*: on the left Perseus and Andromeda, on the right Apollo and Daphne – small figures set in a wide landscape. The window arch depicts the sun-god Phaeton with his chariot.

The decoration of secular rooms with images of the seasons can be found in the Tyrol from the early 15th century (for example at the Torre Aquila in Trent), and by the second half of the 16th century the custom was widespread. Giovanni Paolo Lomazzo's *Treatise on Painting* (Milan 1584) explicitly recommends the months and seasons, annual cycles and triumphal processions for this purpose. The portrayal of the months in the Palazzo delle Albere in Trent (c. 1550–1555), in Beseno Castle (commissioned before 1563

Table organ: songbird inlay with inscription

Table organ (detail): imperial arms, between those of Austria and Tyrol, above Trapp arms held by two putti

by Oswald Trapp I or II), and in the Villa Margone at Ravina, near Trent (before 1566), are above all impressive as landscape pictures, peopled as if incidentally with small figures. Almost contemporary with Churburg (1581–1582) are the paintings of the four seasons and of the triumphal processions of life and death by Orazio and Michele of Brescia in a first-floor reception room at Velthurns Castle, the summer residence of the bishops of Brixen (Bressanone). Here the focal point is men and women engaged in the activities and recreations of the seasons. At Churburg the two aspects are drawn together, with the landscape in the background and attention focused on the allegorical figures with their attributes. As with the fables and mottos on the loggia walls, the didactic purpose of the images is evident – a superimposition that is, if anything, detrimental to their artistic impact. The same might be said of the inscriptions appended to the figures, though these do serve to clarify the puzzle of the latter's reference. The selection of mythological scenes, one may conclude, followed moral as well as humanist educational ideals.

The artist – again probably Paul Nauritius – clearly took Mannerist graphic artworks as his model, although the far-reaching restoration of 1913 again hinders accurate comparison with assured sources. The bold presentation of the sun-god's horses is derived from a fresco by Girolamo Romanino in the Lions' Court of the Castel del Buoncon-

Library

siglio in Trent and confirms the relatedness in that direction. Nevertheless, the scope of the overall concept and – especially in the wood-carving – the excellent workmanship mark Jakob's Room at Churburg as a high-point of secular Tyrolean Mannerism in its own right.

The window sill holds a remarkable early 15th century drinking vessel in the shape of a **griffon's claw**. Made of buffalo horn, it is decorated with gilded silver edgings and stands on three similarly gilded animals' feet. The griffon enters the picture because popular belief held the horn to be a talon of that mythical bird with its legendary properties. Something of a rarity, it is already catalogued in the inventory of 1563. The life-size **wooden sculpture of Jakob VII** (†1563) in everyday dress is unique in the artistic production of the age, as its purpose was not public representation but family piety. It may have been made before Jakob's pilgrimage to the Holy Land to secure his personal memory. The grey felt cape with the badge of the Jerusalem Cross in the showcase next to the figure actually dates from that pilgrimage.

An even rarer item is the **portable table organ** made in 1559 by Michael Strobel from Amberg near

GUIDE TO THE CASTLE

Portrait of Jakob VII (1555)

Braunau on the Inn. The case is finely worked with pilasters, inlaid images, and engraved and gilded copper grilles. The marital arms on the bellows, together with a lengthy Latin inscription, indicate that the work was commissioned by Jakob VII. After painstaking restoration in 1970 by Jürgen Ahrend, the instrument is again playable.

The library itself is not open to visitors, but a glimpse of the interior can be gained through the doorway. The wood-panelled ceiling matches that of Jakob's Room, albeit in simpler form, without the carved rosettes.

Matsch Hall
(18th century)

The late Gothic doorway (1544) bearing the Trapp and Wolkenstein arms leads to a room containing the family archives. An ironclad door and vaulted ceiling serve to protect its irreplaceable contents from theft or damage.

Matsch Hall

Returning to the loggia and taking the stairway to the second floor, one passes a 19th century **Trapp family tree executed on paper** with, at its lower edge, not only the family coat of arms, but also vi-

Portrait of Georg Trapp (1594)

Portrait of Gotthard Trapp
by Oskar Wiedenhofer (1914)

Portrait of Crescentia Trapp
(copy of 1787 original)

Innsbruck – is worthy of special mention. The artist, Josef Anton Kapeller, has succeeded in conveying in a masterly way not only the personal charm of his subject but also the mood of the *ancien regime* on the eve of the French Revolution. Finally, the **life-size portrait of Gotthard Trapp,** painted in 1914 by the Bozen artist Oskar Wiedenhofer, shows the Count in the elegant uniform of an imperial chamberlain. Count Gotthard played an eminent role in the conservation of Churburg Castle. The windows of the hall contain four 16th century roundels with coats of arms – three of the Trapp and one of the Wolkenstein family.

A showcase in the hall contains ancient family treasures, among them a parchment bearing the seal of the Habsburg Archduke Rudolf IV (known as the Founder), who became Tyrolean regent in 1363, confirming in that same year the rights of Ulrich IV von Matsch. Illuminated letters patent of King Ferdinand I, dated 1555, grant Oswald and Jakob Trapp an augmentation of their arms with those of the extinct Matsch line. Two parchment leaves containing a fragment, copied between 1250 and 1350, of Wolfram von Eschenbach's *Willehalm* – a medieval *chanson de geste* – are of great importance for medieval literary history. They were discovered by Count Gotthard in the Churburg archives, where they had been used as a cover for a volume of more recent date. The remains of three sword hilts and a ring were re-

gnettes of several castles in their possession: Lower and Upper Matsch, Churburg, Pisein (Beseno, between Trent and Rovereto), Eschenlohe in Ulten, Campo in Judicaria and the Caldonazzo in Valsugana. Opening directly from the landing, Matsch Hall contains a collection of period furniture and an impressive ancestral portrait gallery, as well as many other objects of interest, under a plain Baroque stucco ceiling. The oldest **portrait**, dated 1555, is of **Jakob VI**; his son Jakob VII is recognizable from the Jerusalem Cross. The life-size portraits of the three Matsch boys **Jakob IX**, **Maximilian** and **Georg Trapp** are by Michael Praun from Mals. That of **Countess Crescentia Trapp** (neé Spaur), dated 1787, although only a copy – the original hangs in Palais Trapp in

GUIDE TO THE CASTLE

Small elevated round-arched entrance to the keep (6th decade, 13th century)

covered from the family tomb in the parish church of Schluderns. Finally, the fragment of a white marble Romanesque capital (c. 1200) was found in 1999 in the course of conservation work on the ruins of Upper Matsch Castle. Decorated with a palmette relief, it has been given a worthy resting place here in Matsch Hall.

Fortifications

A door leads outside from the Baroque hall into the virtually unchanged area of the medieval defensive battlements. The **north curtain wall**, with its wooden walkway, dates back to the original construction period between 1253 and 1259, as does the **castle keep**, at this point still free-standing, whose rough-hewn cornerstones are clearly visible from this elevated position. For defensive reasons the small round-arched door framed in tuff-stone – the only entrance to the massive tower of the keep, whose walls are 2.3 metres thick at the base – was set 8.5 metres above ground. Originally inaccessible from outside, the lower floor was used as a dungeon. Covered wooden stairs lead via a short landing to an iron door decorated with a more recent coat of arms, which opens into the armoury, the most famous feature of Churburg Castle.

Armoury

The armoury as it appears today was installed above the existing stables in the north-eastern corner of the castle by Count Gotthard Trapp in

Wooden landing and staircase to armoury ▷

pp. 50–51:
General view of armoury

1888–1889, since its original quarters to the east of the keep were too crowded. Before commenting upon individual pieces, a word or two should be said about the overall impression of this vaulted room with its more than 300 items of armour and weaponry, many of which come from the foremost production centres north and south of the Alps. Arrayed behind a balustrade and along the walls are the grandest exhibits, while other pieces hang above them. Pride of place is given to two armours of Jakob VI, an ensemble of tournament pieces (garniture) and a **complete armour for man and horse**, with infantry armours around the sides, and a drum of more recent date. The walls hold an important collection of crossbows. The distinctive feature of the Churburg armoury is that it is a dynastic collection, rather than one assembled in modern times, and thus consists entirely of Matsch and Trapp family holdings – the castle's iron wardrobe, so to speak. As early as 1422, a partition agreement between family members stipulated that the family heirlooms remain at Churburg – no wonder, then, that there are pieces here dating back to the 14th century.

Turning now to the most valuable and important items, the oldest of these is a **tournament crest**, probably for a member of the Matsch family, that dates from 1350–70. The pair of horns is made of hardened leather and gesso, painted in a lozenge pattern of green and white, and would have been worn over a great helm. Similar crests are often depicted in 14th-century art, but the original article is extremely rare. The **oldest armour** consists of a segmented breastplate, helmet (a basinet with the snout-like hounskull visor), vambraces (forearm defences) and gauntlets. Some of the elements bear the maker's marks of different Milanese armourers, while the visor is struck with an owner's mark in the shape of the arms of Matsch. Neck, throat and shoulders are protected by mail armour that is attached to the helmet's lower edge. Brass borders inscribed with the biblical text *Iesus autem transiens per medium illorum ibat* (*But Jesus passed through their midst*, Lk 4.30) give the various pieces of plate armour – some of which still retain their original red lining – a strongly decorative tone. Generally dated to 1360–1370 or 1380–1390, the elements of this armour may have been commissioned by Ulrich IV von Matsch, Governor of the Tyrol, who died in 1398.

Imposing even in the Churburg collection is the mid-15th century armour **made for Ulrich IX von Matsch** (1408–1481) by the Milanese master-armourers Pier Innocenzo da Faerno, Antonio Missaglia and Giovanni Negroli. A man of striking stature – the suit stands more than 2 metres tall – Ulrich IX was governor of the Tyrol from 1471–1476. His name is inscribed on the lower leg defences (greaves), while the breastplate bears the Latin mottoes *Ama*

Mounted armour of Jakob VI ▷
by Jörg Seusenhofer, Innsbruck (c. 1540)

Diu (*Love God*) and *Ave domine Jesu Christe ave* (*Hail, Lord Jesus Christ, hail*).

Two armours by the Innsbruck masters Jörg Treytz and Hans Prunner were probably worn by **Gaudenz von Matsch**. They must date from before 1487, when he fell out of favour with Archduke Sigmund.

The earliest Renaissance decoration, comprising etched bands of floral motifs, depictions of saints, and pious inscriptions in Latin, is found on the remains of **two infantry armours** made in Italy c. 1510 by unknown masters. One breastplate shows St. Francis receiving the stigmata, the Madonna and Child, and the martyrdom of St. Sebastian; the other, following a similar pattern, features the Madonna and Child between two angels, flanked by St. Sebastian and St. Barbara with her tower. Such religious decoration was thought to provide its wearer with additional, spiritual protection. On the elevated level, a natural focus of attention is the **complete armour for man and horse** (c. 1540) commissioned by **Jakob VI** from the Innsbruck armourer Jörg Seusenhofer – a unique exhibit in this collection. In front of it is displayed another armour of Jakob VI's, elements from a **tournament garniture** made in Innsbruck by Michael Witz the Younger and decorated by Leonhard Meurl with etched bands of grotesques and floral motifs. Short

◁ Churburg's oldest suit of armour, Milanese workshop (c. 1360–1390)

Armour of Kaspar von Montani (mid-16th century)

inscriptions among the decorations refer to the successful raising of the Turkish siege of Vienna in 1529, and the armour was probably made shortly thereafter in celebration of this momentous event.

Below the raised platform, a showcase contains further treasures. A pair of gauntlets, bearing the mark of the Innsbruck armourer Kaspar Rieder (c. 1480–1485), displays the consummate skill of late Gothic artists: the surfaces are embossed and chased with shallow ridges, edges are decoratively cusped, and the cuffs are adorned with brass borders. Next to them is the pom-

Armour of Ulrich IX von Matsch, Milanese workshop (mid-15th century)

mel of Ulrich IX's sword, and underneath six magnificent saddles.

The breastplate of **Jakob VII's armour** (1553) is etched with a scene showing the count kneeling in front of a large crucifix, as well as his motto *Nusquam tuta fides* (*The faith is nowhere safe*); and, opposite him, the Trapp coat of arms. The armourer responsible for this work is not known with certainty, but the initials MW may refer to the abovementioned Michael Witz. A gilded mace (also visible in the portrait of Jakob VII in Matsch Hall) completes the impressive equipment.

Floral motifs set against a dark background decorate **two elegant ar-**

GUIDE TO THE CASTLE

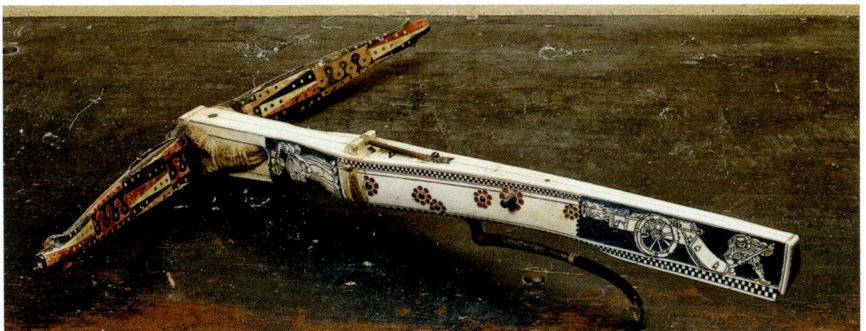

Crossbow (16th century)

mours made in the mid-16th century in Innsbruck. One of them, sporting wild animal masks from helm to knee to enhance the wearer's fearsome appearance, may well be the armour with masks listed in the estate inventory of Jakob VII as belonging to his brother-in-law Kaspar von Montani.

A richly decorated morion (open helmet) of about 1570–1580 is thought to have belonged to either Jakob VIII or his brother Georg III. Etched, gilded and blued, it shows on one side the biblical heroine Judith with the head of Holofernes, and on the other the Roman hero Mucius Scaevola before the Etruscan king Lars Porsena, surrounded by musical instruments and trophies. As before, the blending of humanist education with Mannerist motifs is evident.

Clay cannonballs found in 2001 between curtain wall and round tower facing Schluderns (2nd quarter, 16th century)

Among the weaponry are an impressive number of 16th century **crossbows** with steel bows and wooden stocks, the latter intricately decorated with inlay of polished and engraved staghorn. Especially distinguished among them is one adorned with a large cannon and hunting scene, as well as an exceptionally rare example, actually a combination of a pellet crossbow and a wheellock pistol, that was probably made for Emperor Charles V.

Also noteworthy are the 1250 or so cannon balls that are stored under the wooden benches. Found in 2001 during excavations between the curtain wall and the round artillery tower (known as the "Thurndl"), most are made of fired clay, with some smaller ones of tuff stone. A channel cut in the tower wall allowed them to be rolled down into the building. Dating from the second quarter of the 16th century, they are – especially in this quantity – a rare and important find for the study of early modern artillery.

Hanging from the ceiling is a **green and white silk standard** with the Austrian arms (a red shield with white fess, or central stripe) and the Tyrolean eagle. Commissioned by the Glurns judge Hans Höss in 1607, it was borne by the company mustered by the Glurns court, a right granted in pledge to the Trapp brothers by Emperor Maximilian I in 1517. Among the more recent pieces in the collection is a **heavy armour** made in Augsburg between 1620 and 1630, when the 'golden age' of armour (the 15th and 16th centuries) was rapidly declining. It is thought to have belonged to **Jakob IX**, who was raised to the countship in 1655, or to his brother Georg V.

Madonna and Child, wood
(c. 1270)

◁ Old chapel looking east

GUIDE TO THE CASTLE

Diptych with scenes of the Passion, left panel (2nd decade, 15th century)

Old chapel

The old castle chapel of St. Nicholas, a freestanding building in the southeastern corner of the complex, dates from the earliest phase of construction. The straight-topped **entrance door** with the Matsch arms – exceptionally displaying only one instead of three wings – is in the late Gothic manner. The **interior** consists of two unequally sized rooms, both on an east-west axis, without an apse. The ground plan and the two round-arched windows in the south wall suggest that the south room was the original chapel, the north wall having been removed later and replaced with a massive pillar. The record of a consecration in 1334 sug-

Diptych with scenes of the Passion, right panel (2nd decade, 15th century)

gests that the extension may have been carried out in the first third of the 14th century. The ceiling vault, which springs from the central pillar, probably also dates from that time. The chapel is no longer used for religious services but as an exhibition space for sacred art treasures, a purpose for which it is well suited.

The focal point of the chapel is a **Madonna and Child** on the east wall of the south room. Carved from a single block of wood, the Romanesque work (c. 1270) shows Mary as the new Eve seated in placid majesty, in her right hand an apple, while with the other she holds the child cross-legged on her knee. The arrangement of her cloak

Diptych, outer face, Christ rising from the tomb

is reminiscent of the lower part of a mandorla – the oval aureole frequently found in such images. The Christ Child, as the future Pantocrator, raises his right hand in blessing, while his left holds open the sacred book. The strict frontal aspect of the sculpture is typically Romanesque; the Madonna's headcloth and the niche canopy are, however, early Gothic.

Unlike the sculpture, whose provenance is unclear, the **diptych** standing on the altar is mentioned in the 1563 inventory of Jakob VII's estate. The outside depicts **Christ rising from the tomb** with the instruments of his passion, against the blue background of a starry dawn. The timeless, lyrical mood, emphasized by the double frame with its wealth of intertwining tracery and floral patterns, invites the viewer to devout contemplation. Each inner panel shows six scenes of the **Passion**, from the Last Supper at the top of the left hand panel to the Resurrection at the bottom of the right. The frame and background of this fine artwork are in gold, and the whole has an air of courtly elegance. The corners carry the arms of the bridal couple Elisabeth von Matsch and Friedrich VII von Toggenburg, together with those of their ancestors. Added by a different hand, they document the ownership of the diptych and suggest, therefore, that it only came to Churburg upon Friedrich's death in 1436. Stylistic similarities with miniatures in two illuminated manuscripts of 1414–1415 from the Benedictine abbey of Metten in Lower Bavaria strongly suggest a dating to the second decade of the 15th century. Although the actual artist who made it is not known, the work displays the stylistic characteristics of international Gothic – a blend of Italian, French and Bohemian influences.

In a niche in the south wall is a processional cross from Matsch. A recent addition, its small figure on wide metal arms dates from the early 14th century.

Further artworks are displayed in a showcase in the north room. A small silver chalice (c. 1300) comes from Braunsberg Castle chapel, near Lana, which is dedicated to St. Blaise. It was the custom there, on the feast of the patron saint, to offer the faithful wine from this chalice – the so-called "Blasiusminne" (St.

Processional cross (14th century)

Blaise's kiss) at mass. A late Gothic chalice bears the arms and title of Gaudenz von Matsch, while an 18th century Baroque chalice displays three enamelled medallions. The early Baroque chasuble from Obermatsch Castle is a rare example of silk embroidery on linen: between two angels, the Virgin Mary is crowned by two smaller angels against a setting of flowers arranged in regular groups of three. A late Gothic statue of St. Nicholas, perhaps from a winged altar reredos, is a reminder of the chapel's patron.

On the walls two **memorial shields** tell of a noble funeral. While in the high Middle Ages a nobleman's arms – weapons, helm, shield, sometimes also sword – were hung

Memorial plaque for Georg Trapp (†1525)

above his grave, in the later medieval period the custom of a specifically funerary coat of arms developed. Memorial plaques – wooden roundels bearing an inscription and the carved or painted arms of the deceased – represent a further stage of this development. The two plaques shown here are from the parish church of Besenello, below Pisein (Beseno) Castle, and were made for the funerals of Georg (†1525) and Oswald I (†1560) Trapp. The arms and helm crests are late Gothic, whereas the carved laurel wreath border already reveals the influence of the Renaissance.

New chapel

In 1561 Jakob VII had a **new chapel** built in the free space between the keep and the south curtain wall, probably as an act of thanksgiving for his safe return – no simple matter at the time – from the pilgrimage to Jerusalem undertaken the previous year. The Jerusalem Cross next to the family arms above the chapel entrance commemorates that journey. (This is in fact the third castle chapel: a second, no longer extant building was erected in the 15th century in the north-east corner of the present arcaded courtyard.) Access to the new chapel was originally from the west – i.e. from the arcaded courtyard – but the entrance portal was later moved to its present position. The **keystone** of the white marble arch has four putti holding the Jerusalem Cross and the sword and wheel of the Order of St. Catherine of Mount Sinai, together with the cartouche containing the coat of arms. A Latin inscription states in black lettering the date of the chapel's construction (1561) and proclaims the hereditary rank of major domo conferred on the master of the house. The **vaulted ceiling**, decorated in 1907 in the style of the Tyrolean late Renaissance by Raphael Thaler from Innsbruck, contains – between a pattern of fruits and branches – images of the patron saints of various Trapp family members.

The **Renaissance altar reredos,** with its ornate pilasters and architrave, was completed in 1597 by Michael Praun from Mals. It was commissioned by Jakob VIII, son of the chapel's builder, and his wife, Dorothea Trapp from Pisein. The wing panels show the couple's patron saints on the inside, with the Annunciation to the Virgin Mary on the back. The central image is a

Crucifixion by Rudolf Stolz (1937) on outside wall of new chapel

copy of "St. Mary of the Snows", the famously miraculous painting in Santa Maria Maggiore in Rome – the painting's name is derived from the legendary snowfall of August 5, 356 at the site of the later basilica. Above the architrave two putti hold the marital arms of Trapp-Churburg and Trapp-Pisein, while between them the reredos culminates in a semi-circular depiction of the coronation of the Virgin by Christ and God the Father. Long iron brackets on the wing panels allow the two guardians of the shrine, Sts. Nicholas and George, to be seen even when the triptych is opened. These older, late Gothic figures date from the early 16th century. The predella, with the coats of arms of the bishops of Brixen and Chur at the foot of the pilasters – clear statements of the castle's spiritual affiliation – was added in 1904. The exterior of the chapel has a large mural of the **crucifixion** by the Bozen artist Rudolf Stolz, commissioned in 1937 by Count Gotthard Trapp.

Concluding appraisal

The curtain walls, great hall, chapel and castle keep bear eloquent testimony to the ambitions of the bishops of Chur in establishing, shortly before 1259, the dynastic castle of Churburg.

Its transformation into a Renaissance residence, undertaken in various stages in the course of the 16th century, reached its climax in the arcaded loggia and Jakob's Room. Stone sculptures from the late Gothic and Mannerist periods, together with paintings and wood-carvings, contribute to a unique artistic synthesis whose models range from Ambras Castle, the seat of the Tyrolean regent near Innsbruck, through Buonconsiglio Castle, the bishop's palace in Trent, to the widely printed and diffused Mannerist graphic art of the age.

Bruno Thomas has succinctly characterized the armoury as a unique phenomenon, confined as it is to the possessions of a single family from the 14th to the 17th century. Mario Scalini surmises in this context that Gaudenz von Matsch, realizing in his last years that he would have no male offspring, may have ordered various pieces of armour to be marked with the names of his forebears, to honour their memory. His heirs, the knights, and later counts of the Trapp family have remained faithful to this legacy in exemplary fashion down to the present day.

Literature notes

The entire older literature on Churburg Castle can be found in the most recent monograph: Leo Andergassen: Churburg: Geschichte, Gestalt und Kunst. Photographs Erwin Reiter. Munich and Zurich 1991.

The following articles have appeared subsequently:

Jürg Goll: "Tonkugeln – Spiel oder Krieg". In: 21. Bericht der Stiftung Ziegelei-Museum 2004. Cham 2004, 19–26.

Leo Andergassen: "Das Churburger Passionsdiptychon – eine Stiftung des Friedrich VII. von Toggenburg und der Elisabeth von Matsch". In: M. Giovannoni, L. Deplazes, M. Scalini, H. Theiner, H. Stampfer, L. Andergassen, K. Brandstätter, S. Marseiler: Vogt Gaudenz von Matsch. Ein Tiroler Adeliger zwischen Mittelalter und Neuzeit (Publications of the Südtiroler Kulturinstitut, vol. 3). Bozen 2004, 131–158.

Mario Scalini: "Gaudenz von Matsch, l'armatura e Churburg", in M. Giovannoni, L. Deplazes, M. Scalini, H. Theiner, H. Stampfer, L. Andergassen, K. Brandstätter, S. Marseiler: Vogt Gaudenz von Matsch. Ein Tiroler Adeliger zwischen Mittelalter und Neuzeit (Publications of the Südtiroler Kulturinstitut, vol. 3). Bozen 2004, 63–70.

Timeline

1253	After a feud, Henry IV, bishop of Chur, is granted the right to build a castle or stronghold in the Vinschgau between *Cleven* and *Latsch*.
1259	On Feb. 21 Bishop Henry IV issues the first document bearing the name of his newly built castle, Churburg.
1297	The feudally liege-free lords of Matsch, opponents of the bishops of Chur, gain control of Churburg Castle.
1348	The lords of Matsch declare feudal allegiance to the Tyrolean ruler, Louis of Brandenburg.
1504	Death of Gaudenz von Matsch, last male of the line.
1537	After lengthy disputes Churburg Castle is transferred to the brothers Jakob V, Karl and Georg Trapp, whose mother Barbara is the daughter of Gaudenz von Matsch.
1541	Enfeoffment of the remaining half of Churburg Castle to the Trapp brothers by the Tyrolean ruler. The bishop of Chur had already granted them 'his' half.
1561	Jakob VII builds the new chapel.
1562–1563	Jakob VII has the façade of the dove tower decorated.
1570–1580	Renaissance loggia constructed as an arcaded quadrangle and decorated by *Paul Morizius*.
1576–1580	Jakob's Room fitted out with panelled ceiling, carved door-heads and murals.
1888–1889	Count Gotthard has a new armoury built and the contents of the old armoury transferred.
1960	The old chapel consecrated.
1995	Restoration of loggia murals sponsored by the Messerschmitt Foundation, Munich.

SOUTH TYROL – LAND OF CASTLES

South Tyrolean Castles

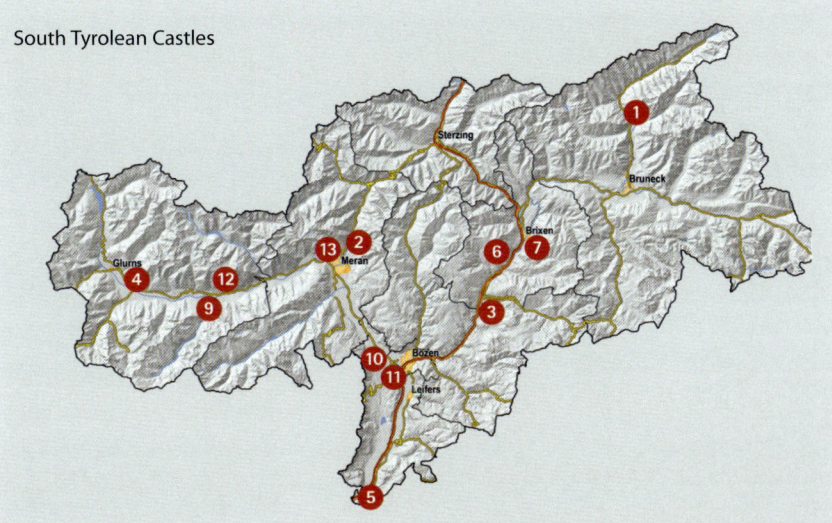

Also available (in German and Italian) in the "Castles" series founded by the Südtiroler Burgeninstitut, Bozen:

Burgen 1
Alexander von Hohenbühel
Taufers (2006)

Burgen 2
Franz Spiegelfeld
Schloss Schenna (2008)

Burgen 3
Alexander von Hohenbühel
Trostburg (2008)

Burgen 4
Helmut Stampfer
Churburg (2009)

Burgen 5
Walter Landi
Haderburg (2010)

Burgen 6
Leo Andergassen
Schloss Velthurns (2010)

Burgen 7
Johann Kronbichler
Hofburg Brixen (2010)

Burgen 9
Leo Andergassen
Montani (2011)

Burgen 10
Walter Landi, Helmut Stampfer, Thomas Steppan
Hocheppan (2011)

Burgen 11
Leo Andergassen, Helmut Stampfer
Burg Sigmundskron (2013)

Burgen 12
Leo Andergassen, Florian Hofer
Kastelbell (2013)

Burgen 13
Leo Andergassen
Schloss Tirol (2015)

SÜDTIROLER BURGENINSTITUT
Obstplatz 25
I-39100 Bozen
Tel./Fax +39 0471 982255
www.burgeninstitut.com

IMPRINT

Guided tours: 20 March until 31 October
Closed: Monday except on bank holidays
Information and group reservation:

Castel Coira
I-39020 Sluderno
T +39 04 73 61 52 41
info@castelcoira.com
www.castelcoira.com

First English edition 2015
© 2015 Verlag Schnell & Steiner GmbH
Leibniz Str. 13, 93055 Regensburg, Germany
Tel. +49-941 787850
Fax +49-941 7878516
Printed by Erhardi Druck GmbH, Regensburg
ISBN 978-3-7954-2998-0

For further information about our publishing programme visit
www.schnell-und-steiner.de
All rights reserved. This book may not be reproduced in whole or in part, either photomechanically or electronically, without the express permission of the publisher.

bliographic information published by the Deutsche Nationalbibliothek
The Deutsche Nationalbibliothek lists this publication in the Deutsche Nationalbibliografie; detailed bibliographic data are available on the Internet at http://dnb.dnb.de.

Front cover
Churburg Castle from the west

Back cover
Loggia

Inside back cover
Ground plan of Churburg Castle

pp. 68–69
Castle keep with later buildings; left foreground: bell tower

Photos and illustrations
Churburg archives: p. 20, inside back cover; Rainer Boos, Alteglofsheim: pp. 17, 29, 30, 31; Erwin Reiter, Haslach: pp. 7, 15, 34, 40, 41, 44, 45, 46, 47, 53, 55, 56, 57 top, 59, 62, 64; Verlag Schnell & Steiner, Regensburg (photo: Johannes Steiner): pp. 60, 61; www.tappeiner.it: front cover, pp.. 4/5, 38, 39, 43, 54, 67, back cover; Autonome Provinz Bozen – Südtirol – Amt für raumbezogene und statische Informatik: p. 71; all other photographs: Anton Brandl, Munich.